Meeting with Jesus

Meeting with Jesus

A Daily Bible Reading Plan for Kids

David Murray

Artwork by Scotty Reifsnyder

CROSSWAY®

WHEATON, ILLINOIS

MEETING WITH JESUS

How many people have you met in your life? Try to count them. Start with your parents, then your brothers and sisters, your neighbors, your friends. Add up those you know from school, church, vacations and so on. What number are you up to? Are you over a hundred yet?

You will meet even more people as you get older, go to different schools, play different sports, move to different houses, and do different jobs. You are going to meet so many people that eventually you will not be able to count them all or remember them all!

There are probably other people you would love to meet but they probably don't want to meet you. Maybe it's an athlete you admire, or a singer, or a businessperson. You think about them and hope one day to meet them, but they don't know you and therefore don't want to meet you.

But there is one person you must meet more than anyone else. And this person wants to meet with you too. And if you meet him, you will never forget him. His name is Jesus, and I want you to meet him because he is the most awesome person you can ever meet.

WHERE DO I MEET JESUS?

If you had been alive about two thousand years ago, you could have met Jesus face-to-face in Israel. But after living there for thirty-three years, he died, rose from the dead, and then went back to heaven. That's where he lives now, reigning and ruling over the whole world.

So how do we meet him today? If he is in heaven and we are on earth, we cannot meet him face-to-face. That's where the Bible comes in. God has designed the Bible so that we can meet Jesus as we read it, hear it preached, and discuss it with others. That's why this book will help you to read the Bible, to hear it preached, and to discuss it with others. My hope and prayer is that in doing so you will meet Jesus in and through the Bible, as millions of others have.

HOW I MET JESUS

To encourage you, let me tell you about how I met Jesus in the Bible. I was born into a Christian family. My parents took me to church and also taught me the Bible at home. However, I did not want to meet Jesus when I was young because I wanted to live my own life without him. Although I went to church, I did not listen very much to the sermons or to my Sunday school teachers. Also, sad to say, I did not read my Bible much.

It's no surprise, then, that I did not meet Jesus. I didn't really want to. I am not proud of that. Indeed, I am ashamed of it and often wish I could live my childhood and teen years all over again.

But Jesus did not give up on me. Even though I did not want to meet him, he wanted to meet me. In my early twenties, my life was not going well. I was trying to live without Jesus and I was very unhappy. After some sad events in my life, I went home to my parents, and they talked to me about how I needed to meet Jesus. My mom gave me a book to help me study the Bible, and I started reading it carefully for the first time. My prayer as I opened my Bible was, "Lord, please show me Jesus."

Jesus Lives in the Bible

Almost immediately I was amazed at how Jesus began to pop out of the pages of the Bible. The book that I had thought was so boring was now alive and exciting. I wasn't reading a lifeless book; I was meeting a living person. Every day I learned more and more about this lovely person, Jesus Christ. As I did so, Jesus became more and more real, clear, and present to me. Soon, he was as real to me as my mom and dad!

As I read my Bible each day and met Jesus in its pages, I was sure I was hearing his voice speaking directly to me in the words I was reading. It then felt normal and natural to start speaking back to him in prayer and talking to him about my life.

Jesus Lives in Sermons

I started listening to my pastor's sermons with new attention. Again, Jesus came alive in the sermons. I was not just listening to my pastor; I was listening to my Jesus, and I was loving him more and more—so much so that I couldn't wait for next Sunday and started listening to recorded sermons from other preachers in my car on weekdays. I sometimes felt as if Jesus were in the passenger seat beside me chatting to me through the sermons.

Jesus Lives in Christians

I couldn't keep all this to myself and started going to homes where I knew other Christians who loved Jesus would meet and talk about him. I listened with amazement as they spoke about Jesus as a living person in their own lives too. I had many questions, and these Christian friends patiently answered them week after week. And as they did so, it was as if Jesus were in the room with us, as one of our friends. We also memorized Scripture verses about Jesus and challenged one another to recite them. Those were such happy, happy times.

Jesus Lives Today

Now, thirty years later, Jesus is more real and precious to me than ever before, and that's why I'm so excited for you to meet him early in life rather than wasting years like I did. I've therefore written this Bible reading plan to help you meet Jesus in Bible reading, in listening to sermons about the Bible, and in discussing the Bible with others.

The Bible reading plan is divided up into small daily portions to make it easy for you to digest. Each reading has a title and a question to help you think about what you are reading. In the course of a year this will take you through the whole life of Christ as found in the Gospel of Luke. I've chosen the readings so that you can follow the life of Christ more or less in the order it happened. I've therefore added some readings from the other Gospels to fill out some of the places that Luke does not cover.

On Sunday, I haven't given you a Bible reading. That's partly to help you catch up if you missed any days. But it's also to help you focus on meeting Jesus by listening to the sermon you hear in church and by discussing a question about your reading with your dad or mom, or maybe another Christian friend. You can also use Sunday to practice your weekly memory verse.

Show Me Jesus

You can fill in the section for prayer points each week with specific prayer needs that you want to remember as you talk to Jesus. But the biggest prayer of all that I want you to keep praying as you go through this book is "Show me Jesus!" If you do, he will meet with you and come alive in your life in an unforgettable way.

David Murray

PS If you want to find out more about the Bible, you can also use *Exploring the Bible: A Bible Reading Plan for Kids*. It's another one-year daily Bible reading plan that covers the most important chapters in the Bible, from Genesis to Revelation. You can also view short videos to supplement each week's readings in *Exploring the Bible* and *Meeting Jesus* at http://head hearthand.org/bibleexplorer.

MEETING 1 | JOHN THE BAPTIST IS BORN

We can tell how important a person is by how much effort is made to prepare for his or her arrival. This week, we will read about how God arranged a careful writer, a childless couple, an angel, and a special baby named John to prepare the way for Jesus.

 ## TALKING TO JESUS: PRAYER POINTS

We are going to be hearing Jesus's voice as we read the Bible, but he wants to hear your voice too. So, each week write down two or three prayer requests and pray for them during the week.

 ## REMEMBERING JESUS: MEMORY VERSE | LUKE 1:16

To help you remember each week's meeting with Jesus, I've chosen a verse for you to memorize. Try to repeat it out loud a few times a day, and then test yourself to see if you can say it without looking at the verse.

MONDAY | A Careful Writer

 Luke 1:1–4

 Answer:

 Who wrote this book about Jesus? (Hint: look at the title of the Gospel.)

TUESDAY | A Childless Couple

 Luke 1:5–7

Answer:

 Describe Zechariah (some Bibles call him Zacharias) and Elizabeth (v. 6).

WEDNESDAY | An Awesome Angel

 Luke 1:8–12

Answer:

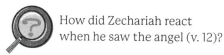 How did Zechariah react when he saw the angel (v. 12)?

THURSDAY | A Preparer of People

 Luke 1:13–17

 John prepared people for
_____ (v. 17).

Answer:

FRIDAY | A Lack of Faith

 Luke 1:18–22

 Zechariah was unable to
speak because he did not
b_____ (v. 20).

Answer:

SATURDAY | A Baby from the Lord

 Luke 1:23–25

 What did God take away
from Elizabeth (v. 25)?

Answer:

SUNDAY | MEETING JESUS WITH OTHERS

The three most common ways that people meet Jesus are reading about him in the Bible, talking with others about him, and listening to sermons about him. This week we read about him in the Bible. Today, we want to meet him by talking with others about him and by listening to sermons about him.

Each Sunday you will find a question that you can talk about with your parents, your pastor, or your Sunday school teacher. There is also space for you to write about what you heard in the sermon—especially what you learned about Jesus.

 ## TALKING ABOUT JESUS

John prepared the way for Jesus to come into the world. How can you prepare the way for Jesus to come into your heart?

 ## LISTENING TO JESUS

Sermon Title

Sermon Verse

Sermon Notes

What did you learn about Jesus today in church?

MEETING 2 | JESUS IS JOY

This week we will see how Jesus brought joy to the world even before he was born. Jesus's mother rejoiced over him, and John the Baptist rejoiced when he "met" Jesus for the first time.

 TALKING TO JESUS: PRAYER POINTS

 REMEMBERING JESUS: MEMORY VERSE | LUKE 1:47

MONDAY | Jesus Makes Mary Happy

 Luke 1:26–33

Answer:

 What will Jesus be called (v. 32)?

TUESDAY | Jesus's Birth Is Explained

 Luke 1:34–38

Answer:

 What's another name Jesus will be called (v. 35)?

WEDNESDAY | Jesus Makes John Happy

 Luke 1:39–45

Write the verse:

 Luke 1:45

THURSDAY | Jesus Is Mary's Happy Song

 Luke 1:46–50

 What did Mary call God (v. 47)?

Answer:

FRIDAY | Jesus Turns the World Upside Down

 Luke 1:51–56

 Luke 1:52

Write the verse:

SATURDAY | Jesus's Cousin Is Born

 Luke 1:57–58, 76–80

 What will John the Baptist do (v. 77)?

Answer:

SUNDAY | MEETING JESUS WITH OTHERS

 ## TALKING ABOUT JESUS

John the Baptist jumped in the womb when he heard the voice of Jesus's mother (Luke 1:41). Mary rejoiced when she thought about her son as her Savior (Luke 1:47). Why does Jesus make people happy? How does Jesus make you happy?

 ## LISTENING TO JESUS

Sermon Title

Sermon Verse

Sermon Notes

What did you learn about Jesus today in church?

MEETING 3 | JESUS ARRIVES

God promised Jesus and then prepared for Jesus. This week you will read about Jesus arriving in the world and how different people reacted when they met him for the first time.

 TALKING TO JESUS: PRAYER POINTS

 REMEMBERING JESUS: MEMORY VERSE | LUKE 2:11

MONDAY | Jesus Is Born

 Luke 2:1–7

Answer:

 Why did Mary lay Jesus in a manger (v. 7)?

TUESDAY | Jesus Praised by Angels

 Luke 2:8–14

Answer:

 What did the angels say to the shepherds (v. 11)?

WEDNESDAY | Jesus Visited by Shepherds

 Luke 2:15–20

Answer:

 What did the shepherds do when they saw Jesus (v. 20)?

THURSDAY | Jesus Brought to Temple

 Luke 2:21–24

 Jesus was presented to
_____ (v. 22).

Answer:

FRIDAY | Jesus Welcomed by Simeon

 Luke 2:25–35

 What did Simeon see when
he saw Jesus (v. 30)?

Answer:

SATURDAY | Jesus Welcomed by Anna

 Luke 2:36–40

 Describe Jesus as
a child (v. 40).

Answer:

SUNDAY | MEETING JESUS WITH OTHERS

 ## TALKING ABOUT JESUS

After Anna met Jesus for the first time, she went out and spoke to many people about him (Luke 2:38). Who will you speak to about Jesus, and how will you do it?

Sermon Title

Sermon Verse

Sermon Notes

What did you learn about Jesus today in church?

MEETING 4 | THE KING OF KINGS GROWS UP

This week we will meet Jesus as a child, first as an infant being protected from an evil king, and then, at age twelve, teaching the temple teachers.

 ## TALKING TO JESUS: PRAYER POINTS

 ## REMEMBERING JESUS: MEMORY VERSE | LUKE 2:52

MONDAY | Jesus Visited by Wise Men

 Matthew 2:1–6

Answer:

 Why did the wise men come to Jerusalem (v. 2)?

TUESDAY | Jesus Protected by the Wise Men

 Matthew 2:7–12

Answer:

 How did the wise men react when they met Jesus (v. 11)?

WEDNESDAY | Jesus Protected by His Father

 Matthew 2:19–23

Answer:

 Where did Joseph protect Jesus? E_____ (v. 19) and N_____ (v. 23).

THURSDAY | Jesus Goes Missing

 Luke 2:41–46

 What was Jesus doing in the temple (v. 46)?

Answer:

FRIDAY | Jesus Is Found

 Luke 2:47–50

 How did people react to Jesus's teaching (v. 47)?

Answer:

SATURDAY | Jesus Grows in Every Way

 Luke 2:51–52

 How did Jesus respond to his parents (v. 51)?

Answer:

SUNDAY | MEETING JESUS WITH OTHERS

 ## TALKING ABOUT JESUS

As you learned in your memory verse this week, Jesus grew in wisdom and in favor with God and others (Luke 2:52). How can you grow like this?

 ## LISTENING TO JESUS

Sermon Title

Sermon Verse

Sermon Notes

What did you learn about Jesus today in church?

MEETING 5 | JESUS IS TEMPTED

Up until now Jesus mostly grew up in private. That all changed when John the Baptist publicly announced him at his baptism. This also attracted the attention of the devil, who started attacking him in the desert.

 TALKING TO JESUS: PRAYER POINTS

 REMEMBERING JESUS: MEMORY VERSE | JOHN 1:29

MONDAY | Jesus Will Save

 Luke 3:1–6

Answer:

 What did John preach (v. 6)?

TUESDAY | Jesus and Repentance

 Luke 3:7–14

Answer:

 What kind of fruits were the people to produce (v. 8)?

WEDNESDAY | Jesus Greater Than John the Baptist

 Luke 3:15–18

Answer:

 What did John say about Jesus's sandals (v. 16)?

THURSDAY | Jesus Is Baptized

 John 1:29–34

 What did John call Jesus (v. 29)?

Answer:

FRIDAY | Jesus Is Tempted

 Luke 4:1–8

 Who are we to worship and serve (v. 8)?

Answer:

SATURDAY | Jesus Beats Temptation

 Luke 4:9–15

 What did the devil do when Jesus beat his temptations (v. 13)?

Answer:

SUNDAY | MEETING JESUS WITH OTHERS

 ## TALKING ABOUT JESUS

Jesus beat the devil's temptations by speaking the Bible to him (Luke 4:4, 8, 12). What Bible verses can help you beat the devil's temptations?

 ## LISTENING TO JESUS

Sermon Title

Sermon Verse

Sermon Notes

What did you learn about Jesus today in church?

MEETING 6 | JESUS CALLS

This week we meet Jesus giving a number of calls. He calls disciples to follow him, he calls Nathanael to trust him, he calls for a clean temple, he calls for new birth, and he calls to faith. Try to hear Jesus calling you as you meet him this week.

 TALKING TO JESUS: PRAYER POINTS

 REMEMBERING JESUS: MEMORY VERSE | JOHN 3:16

MONDAY | Jesus Calls His First Disciples

 John 1:35–42

Answer:

 What did the disciples do when they heard Jesus speak (v. 37)?

TUESDAY | Jesus Calls Nathanael

 John 1:43–49

Answer:

 What did Nathanael call Jesus (v. 49)?

WEDNESDAY | Jesus Performs His First Miracle

 John 2:1–11

Answer:

 What did the disciples do when they saw Jesus's first miracle (v. 11)?

THURSDAY | Jesus Calls for a Pure Temple

 John 2:13–17

 What did Jesus call the temple? My F_____ h_____ (v. 16).

Answer:

FRIDAY | Jesus Calls for New Birth

 John 3:1–8

 Jesus said, "You must be _____ _____ (v. 7).

Answer:

SATURDAY | Jesus Calls to Faith

 John 3:10–17

 What happens if we believe in Jesus (v. 15)?

Answer:

SUNDAY | MEETING JESUS WITH OTHERS

 ## TALKING ABOUT JESUS

Jesus calls us to believe in him (John 3:16). What does it mean to believe in Jesus? Are you hearing that call? If so, what are you doing about it?

 ## LISTENING TO JESUS

Sermon Title

Sermon Verse

Sermon Notes

What did you learn about Jesus today in church?

MEETING 7 | JESUS REFRESHES

One of the best feelings in the world is drinking a cool glass of pure water after working hard or playing a sport on a hot summer's day. It refreshes us and gives us new life. This week we will see how Jesus refreshes and gives new life to a sinful woman whom he met in a dry and dusty desert.

TALKING TO JESUS: PRAYER POINTS

REMEMBERING JESUS: MEMORY VERSE | JOHN 4:29

MONDAY | Jesus Is the Bridegroom

 John 3:25–30

Answer:

 What did John say
about Jesus (v. 30)?

TUESDAY | Jesus Gives Everlasting Life

 John 3:31–36

Answer:

 What do you have if you
believe in Jesus (the
Son of God) (v. 36)?

WEDNESDAY | Jesus Meets a Samaritan Woman

 John 4:1–8

Answer:

 What did Jesus seek from
the Samaritan woman (v. 7)?

THURSDAY | Jesus Offers Living Water

 John 4:9–15

 What kind of water did Jesus offer the Samaritan woman (v. 10)?

Answer:

FRIDAY | Jesus Convicts of Sin

 John 4:16–26

 How are we to worship God (v. 24)?

Answer:

SATURDAY | Jesus Saves the Samaritan Woman

 John 4:28–30, 39–42

 What did the Samaritans call Jesus (v. 42)?

Answer:

SUNDAY | MEETING JESUS WITH OTHERS

 ## TALKING ABOUT JESUS

John wrote forty-two verses about the meeting between Jesus and the Samaritan woman. What did you learn about Jesus from this lengthy meeting?

LISTENING TO JESUS

Sermon Title

Sermon Verse

Sermon Notes

What did you learn about Jesus today in church?

MEETING 8 | JESUS CASTS OUT A DEVIL

One of the hardest sermons I ever preached was the first time I preached in the congregation I grew up in. It was difficult for me, but it was also difficult for people who had known me from very young to listen to me as a preacher. We're about to hear the first sermon Jesus preached when he went back to his hometown of Nazareth. Notice also how Jesus's powerful word casts out a devil.

TALKING TO JESUS: PRAYER POINTS

REMEMBERING JESUS: MEMORY VERSE | LUKE 4:18
(If this verse is too long for you, just memorize part of it.)

MONDAY | Jesus Preaches at Nazareth

 Luke 4:16–19

Answer:

 What did Jesus proclaim or preach in this sermon (v. 18)?

TUESDAY | Jesus Amazes His Hearers

 Luke 4:20–22

Answer:

 What amazed people about Jesus (v. 22)?

WEDNESDAY | Jesus Challenges His Hearers

 Luke 4:23–27

Answer:

 What did Jesus expect the people of Nazareth to say to him (v. 23)?

THURSDAY | Jesus Is Opposed

 Luke 4:28–32

 Why were people astonished at Jesus's teaching (v. 32)?

Answer:

FRIDAY | Jesus Casts Out an Evil Spirit

 Luke 4:33–37

 What did the people say about Jesus (v. 36)?

Answer:

SATURDAY | Jesus Heals Many

 Luke 4:38–44

 What did Jesus preach (v. 43)?

Answer:

SUNDAY | MEETING JESUS WITH OTHERS

 ## TALKING ABOUT JESUS

Your memory verse for this week, Luke 4:18, describes the impact of Jesus's ministry. In what ways has Jesus changed you? Ask others how Jesus has changed them.

LISTENING TO JESUS

Sermon Title

Sermon Verse

Sermon Notes

What did you learn about Jesus today in church?

MEETING 9 | JESUS CALLS FISHERMEN

Jesus is interested in every area of our lives. He's not just concerned about spiritual or churchy things. He's also fascinated with what we do from Monday to Saturday, our hobbies, our sports, our work. Here we will meet Jesus both fishing and forgiving.

 TALKING TO JESUS: PRAYER POINTS

 REMEMBERING JESUS: MEMORY VERSE | LUKE 5:32

MONDAY | Jesus Catches Fish

 Luke 5:1–7

Answer:

 What happened to the fishing boats when Jesus went fishing (v.7)?

TUESDAY | Jesus Calls Fishermen

 Luke 5:8–11

Answer:

 What will Peter catch from now on (v. 10)?

WEDNESDAY | Jesus Heals a Leper

 Luke 5:12–16

Answer:

 What did Jesus say to the leper (v. 13)?

THURSDAY | Jesus Forgives Sin

 Luke 5:17–20

 What did Jesus say to the lame man (v. 20)?

Answer:

FRIDAY | Jesus Heals a Lame Man

 Luke 5:21–26

 What did the people say when Jesus healed the lame man (v. 26)?

Answer:

SATURDAY | Jesus Calls a Tax Collector

 Luke 5:27–32

 Who needs a physician (a doctor) (v. 31)?

Answer:

SUNDAY | MEETING JESUS WITH OTHERS

 ## TALKING ABOUT JESUS

Jesus said he came as a doctor to heal the sick (Luke 5:31). What is the worst sickness and how can Jesus cure it?

 ## LISTENING TO JESUS

Sermon Title

Sermon Verse

Sermon Notes

What did you learn about Jesus today in church?

MEETING 10 | JESUS RULES AND HEALS

This week we will meet Jesus as Lord. He reigns and rules over the Sabbath, over his disciples, and over blessings, and he heals disease and disability.

 TALKING TO JESUS: PRAYER POINTS

 REMEMBERING JESUS: MEMORY VERSE | LUKE 6:5

MONDAY | Jesus Is Lord of the Sabbath

 Luke 6:1–5

Answer:

 What does Jesus call himself in verse 5? The S____ of M_____.

TUESDAY | Jesus Is Lord over Disability

 Luke 6:6–11

Answer:

 What question did Jesus ask the Pharisees (v. 9)?

WEDNESDAY | Jesus Is Lord of His Disciples

 Luke 6:12–16

Answer:

 What did Jesus do the night before he chose his disciples (v. 12)?

THURSDAY | Jesus Is Lord over Disease

 Luke 6:17–19

 How many people did Jesus heal (v. 19)?

Answer:

FRIDAY | Jesus Is Lord in His Blessings (1)

 Matthew 5:1–6

 Who has the kingdom of heaven (v. 3)?

Answer:

SATURDAY | Jesus Is Lord in His Blessings (2)

 Matthew 5:7–12

 Who will see God (v. 8)?

Answer:

SUNDAY | MEETING JESUS WITH OTHERS

 ## TALKING ABOUT JESUS

This week we saw Jesus ruling as Lord in many different areas of life. In what ways can you show Jesus is Lord over your life? What areas of your life do you not want Jesus to rule over?

 ## LISTENING TO JESUS

Sermon Title

Sermon Verse

Sermon Notes

What did you learn about Jesus today in church?

MEETING 11 | JESUS LOVES

What does Jesus love? This week's meetings with Jesus will highlight how Jesus loves mercy, God, prayer, good trees, and doers of his Word. But we also discover that he hates hypocrisy.

 ### TALKING TO JESUS: PRAYER POINTS

 ### REMEMBERING JESUS: MEMORY VERSE | LUKE 6:35

MONDAY | Jesus Loves Mercy

 Luke 6:27–31

Answer:

 What are we to do to our
personal enemies (v. 27)?

TUESDAY | Jesus Commands Us to Love Like God

 Luke 6:32–36

Answer:

 Who is our model for
mercy (v. 36)?

WEDNESDAY | Jesus Hates Hypocrisy

 Luke 6:37–42

Answer:

 What should you remove
from your eye (v. 42)?

THURSDAY | Jesus Loves Prayer

 Matthew 6:8–14

 Who are we to pray to (v. 9)?

Answer:

FRIDAY | Jesus Loves Good Trees

 Luke 6:43–45

 Where do our words come from (v. 45)?

Answer:

SATURDAY | Jesus Loves Doers of His Word

 Luke 6:46–49

 What happens if we listen to but do not obey God's Word (v. 49)?

Answer:

SUNDAY | MEETING JESUS WITH OTHERS

 ## TALKING ABOUT JESUS

How can you love like Jesus loved? How can you show his love to your family, to your friends, and even to kids who don't like you?

 ## LISTENING TO JESUS

Sermon Title

Sermon Verse

Sermon Notes

What did you learn about Jesus today in church?

MEETING 12 | JESUS SURPRISES

Jesus was full of surprises. Not funny surprises, but unexpected words and actions. For example, this week he will surprise us with his view on who had the greatest faith in Israel. He will surprise us by raising a dead boy back to life. He will surprise us by challenging John the Baptist to keep believing in him. He will surprise us by who he invites to come to him.

 TALKING TO JESUS: PRAYER POINTS

 REMEMBERING JESUS: MEMORY VERSE | MATTHEW 11:28

MONDAY | Jesus Hears a Centurion's Prayer

 Luke 7:1–5

Answer:

 Describe the centurion (v. 5).

TUESDAY | Jesus Heals a Centurion's Servant

 Luke 7:6–10

Answer:

 What did Jesus say about the centurion's faith (v. 9)?

WEDNESDAY | Jesus Raises a Widow's Son

 Luke 7:11–17

Answer:

 Who did the people say had visited them (v. 16)?

THURSDAY | Jesus Assures John the Baptist

 Luke 7:18–23

 Who is blessed (v. 23)?

Answer:

FRIDAY | Jesus Curses Cities

 Matthew 11:20–24

 Why did Jesus rebuke the cities (v. 20)?

Answer:

SATURDAY | Jesus Invites Sinners

 Matthew 11:25–30

 Who does Jesus invite to come to him (v. 28)?

Answer:

SUNDAY | MEETING JESUS WITH OTHERS

 ## TALKING ABOUT JESUS

What about Jesus has surprised you most? Ask others what surprised them as they got to know Jesus.

 ## LISTENING TO JESUS

Sermon Title

Sermon Verse

Sermon Notes

What did you learn about Jesus today in church?

MEETING 13 | JESUS SOWS

This week we will meet Jesus sowing seed in a field. This is perhaps the best-known parable in the Bible and teaches the importance of not just listening to Jesus but also believing in him and obeying him. He underlines this parable by saying his true family are those who do his Word (Luke 8:21).

 TALKING TO JESUS: PRAYER POINTS

 REMEMBERING JESUS: MEMORY VERSE | LUKE 8:18

MONDAY | Jesus Is Anointed

 Luke 7:36–39

Answer:

 Why was the Pharisee angry with Jesus (v. 39)?

TUESDAY | Jesus Explains Love

 Luke 7:40–43

Answer:

 What did the moneylender do when the men could not pay him back (v. 42)?

WEDNESDAY | Jesus Forgives Sin

 Luke 7:44–50

Answer:

 The saved woman was to go in _____ (v. 50).

THURSDAY | Jesus Tells the Parable of the Sower

 Luke 8:4–10

 Describe the four kinds of ground in this parable (vv. 5–8).

 Answer:

FRIDAY | Jesus Explains the Parable of the Sower

 Luke 8:11–15

 What is the seed in this parable (v. 11)?

Answer:

SATURDAY | Jesus Identifies His Family

 Luke 8:16–21

 Who are Jesus's mother and brothers (v. 21)?

 Answer:

SUNDAY | MEETING JESUS WITH OTHERS

TALKING ABOUT JESUS

Think about the four kinds of hearer (Luke 8:12–15). What kind of hearer are you?

LISTENING TO JESUS

Sermon Title

Sermon Verse

Sermon Notes

What did you learn about Jesus today in church?

MEETING 14 | JESUS TELLS STORIES

Last week Jesus told us the story about the sower, the seed, and the soils. This week he tells us more stories with spiritual lessons. The first one finds him back in the field, this time among weeds (also known as *tares*).

 TALKING TO JESUS: PRAYER POINTS

 REMEMBERING JESUS: MEMORY VERSE | MATTHEW 13:43

MONDAY | Jesus Tells the Parable of the Weeds

 Matthew 13:24–30

Answer:

 Who sowed the weeds or tares (v. 28)?

TUESDAY | Jesus Explains the Parable of the Weeds

 Matthew 13:36–43

Answer:

 Who is the enemy (v. 39)?

WEDNESDAY | Jesus Tells the Parables of the Mustard Seed and the Leaven

Answer:

 Matthew 13:31–35

 What happened to the mustard seed (v. 32)?

THURSDAY | Jesus Tells the Parables of the Treasure and the Pearl

 Matthew 13:44–46

 What did the treasure-finder and the pearl-finder do? They sold_____ (vv. 44, 46).

Answer:

FRIDAY | Jesus Tells the Parable of the Net

 Matthew 13:47–50

 Where will the wicked be cast (v. 50)?

Answer:

SATURDAY | Jesus Tells the Parable of the House Owner

 Matthew 13:51–54

 What does the master of the house do (v. 52)?

Answer:

SUNDAY | MEETING JESUS WITH OTHERS

 ## TALKING ABOUT JESUS

Not all of Jesus's stories have a happy ending. In the parable of the weeds and the parable of the net the wicked end up being burned in the fire of hell. Why does Jesus tell people such sad stories?

LISTENING TO JESUS

Sermon Title

Sermon Verse

Sermon Notes

What did you learn about Jesus today in church?

MEETING 15 | JESUS CLEANSES AND HEALS

This week, we will meet Jesus healing his fearful disciples, a demon-possessed man, a sick woman, and a dead girl.

 TALKING TO JESUS: PRAYER POINTS

 REMEMBERING JESUS: MEMORY VERSE | LUKE 8:48

MONDAY | Jesus Stills the Storm

 Luke 8:22–25

Answer:

 What did Jesus ask the disciples (v. 25)?

TUESDAY | Jesus Meets a Demon-Possessed Man

 Luke 8:26–31

Answer:

 Why was the man called Legion (v. 30)?

WEDNESDAY | Jesus Heals a Demon-Possessed Man

 Luke 8:32–36

Answer:

 Describe the healed man (v. 35).

THURSDAY | Jesus Disciples a Demon-Possessed Man

 Luke 8:37–39

Answer:

 What did Jesus tell the healed man to do (v. 39)?

FRIDAY | Jesus Heals a Woman

 Luke 8:43–48

Answer:

 How was the woman healed or made whole (v. 48)?

SATURDAY | Jesus Heals a Girl

 Luke 8:40–42, 49–56

Answer:

 What did Jesus ask the girl's parents to do (v. 50)?

SUNDAY | MEETING JESUS WITH OTHERS

 ## TALKING ABOUT JESUS

Jesus told the healed man to return to his hometown and tell everyone about what great things God had done for him (Luke 8:39). What great things has God done for you, and who are you telling about it?

LISTENING TO JESUS

Sermon Title

Sermon Verse

Sermon Notes

What did you learn about Jesus today in church?

MEETING 16 | JESUS SUPPLIES

This week we will meet Jesus as he supplies great needs. He supplied the great spiritual needs of the world by providing the gospel. He supplied the great physical needs of the hungry by providing food. He supplied the great emotional needs of the disciples by calming their fear.

 TALKING TO JESUS: PRAYER POINTS

 REMEMBERING JESUS: MEMORY VERSE | MATTHEW 14:27

MONDAY | Jesus Sends Out Disciples

 Luke 9:1–6

Answer:

 What did the disciples do (v. 6)?

TUESDAY | Jesus Feared by Herod

 Luke 9:7–9

Answer:

 What did Herod think when he heard about Jesus (v. 7)?

WEDNESDAY | Jesus Sees Hungry Crowds

 Luke 9:10–13

Answer:

 How much food did Jesus and the disciples have (v. 13)?

THURSDAY | Jesus Feeds the Hungry Crowd

 Luke 9:14–17

 How many were fed (v. 14)?

Answer:

FRIDAY | Jesus Comes in a Storm

 Matthew 14:22–27

 What did Jesus say to his disciples (v. 27)?

Answer:

SATURDAY | Jesus Calms a Storm

 Matthew 14:28–33

 What did the worshipers say (v. 33)?

Answer:

SUNDAY | MEETING JESUS WITH OTHERS

 ## TALKING ABOUT JESUS

Jesus supplied many needs in this week's readings. What needs do you have and how might Jesus supply them? How can Jesus meet the needs of other people you know?

LISTENING TO JESUS

Sermon Title

Sermon Verse

Sermon Notes

What did you learn about Jesus today in church?

MEETING 17 | JESUS REBUKES

Jesus did not only speak loving words of grace to the needy but also painful words of rebuke to the proud. In this meeting, Jesus rebukes the proud Pharisees again and again.

 TALKING TO JESUS: PRAYER POINTS

 REMEMBERING JESUS: MEMORY VERSE | MATTHEW 15:25

MONDAY | Jesus and Honoring Parents

 Matthew 15:1–9

Answer:

 They honored God with their _____ but their _____ were far from him (v. 8).

TUESDAY | Jesus and Washing Hands

 Matthew 15:10–14

Answer:

 What defiles a person (v. 11)?

WEDNESDAY | Jesus and Washing of the Heart

Answer:

 Matthew 15:15–20

 What comes out of the heart (v. 19)?

THURSDAY | Jesus Heals a Young Woman

 Matthew 15:21–28

 Answer:

 What did the woman say to Jesus (v. 25)?

FRIDAY | Jesus Rebukes Pharisees

 Matthew 16:1–4

Answer:

 What did the Pharisees and Sadducees ask for (v. 1)?

SATURDAY | Jesus Warns about the Pharisees

 Matthew 16:5–12

Answer:

 What did Jesus warn the people about (v. 12)?

SUNDAY | MEETING JESUS WITH OTHERS

 ## TALKING ABOUT JESUS

The Jesus we met this week had many warnings for the proud. However, he also met and helped the helpless by healing the daughter of a humble woman. Her prayer was your memory verse this week (Matt. 15:25). Ask the Christians you know when and how many times a day they pray this prayer.

 ## LISTENING TO JESUS

Sermon Title

Sermon Verse

Sermon Notes

What did you learn about Jesus today in church?

MEETING 18 | JESUS FIRST

Who is the greatest? That's a question many ask and argue about. Even the disciples argued about it because some of them wanted to be the greatest. This week's readings supply the only true answer—Jesus is the greatest. We see that in Peter's confession of Jesus, in the transfiguration of Jesus, and in his healing of a boy that the disciples could not help.

TALKING TO JESUS: PRAYER POINTS

REMEMBERING JESUS: MEMORY VERSE | LUKE 9:48

MONDAY | Jesus Is Confessed

 Luke 9:18–22

Answer:

 What did Peter call Jesus (v. 20)?

TUESDAY | Jesus Calls to Cross-Bearing

 Luke 9:23–27

Answer:

 What are Jesus's followers to take up (v. 23)?

WEDNESDAY | Jesus Transfigured (Changed in Appearance)

 Luke 9:28–36

Answer:

 What did the voice from heaven say (v. 35)?

THURSDAY | Jesus Heals a Demon-Possessed Boy

 Luke 9:37–42

 How did Jesus describe the people (v. 41)?

Answer:

FRIDAY | Jesus Teaches about True Greatness

 Luke 9:43–48

 What is the way to be great (v. 48)?

Answer:

SATURDAY | Jesus Rejects Excuses

 Luke 9:57–62

 Luke 9:62

Write the verse:

SUNDAY | MEETING JESUS WITH OTHERS

TALKING ABOUT JESUS

As your memory verse taught you this week (Luke 9:48), the way to Christlike greatness is to be the least, the way to power is to serve. What can you do this week to be the least and to serve?

LISTENING TO JESUS

Sermon Title

Sermon Verse

Sermon Notes

What did you learn about Jesus today in church?

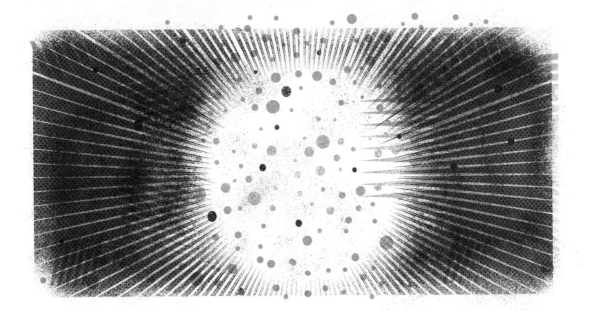

MEETING 19 | JESUS ENLIGHTENS

In last week's meeting, Jesus traveled to Jerusalem (Luke 9:51). Now we find him in Jerusalem. Jerusalem was a spiritually dark city but Christ shone in it as a bright light by forgiving sin, by delivering slaves to sin, and by giving a blind man sight.

 TALKING TO JESUS: PRAYER POINTS

 REMEMBERING JESUS: MEMORY VERSE | JOHN 8:12

MONDAY | Jesus Promises the Holy Spirit

 John 7:37–39

Answer:

 Jesus uses water as a picture of the H_____ S_____ (v. 39).

TUESDAY | Jesus Divides His Hearers

 John 7:40–46

Answer:

 Some people thought Jesus was the P_____. Others thought he was the C_____ (v. 40, 41).

WEDNESDAY | Jesus Forgives Immorality

 John 8:3–11

Answer:

 What did Jesus say to the woman (v. 11)?

THURSDAY | Jesus Is the Light of the World

John 8:12–14

If a person follows Christ, he
will not walk in d_____
but in the l_____ (v. 12).

Answer:

FRIDAY | Jesus Delivers Slaves

John 8:31–38

What will the truth do (v. 32)?

Answer:

SATURDAY | Jesus Gives the Blind Their Sight

John 9:1–7

Why was the man
born blind (v. 3)?

Answer:

SUNDAY | MEETING JESUS WITH OTHERS

 ## TALKING ABOUT JESUS

How does Jesus bring light into your life? How can you shine light into the world like Jesus did?

 ## LISTENING TO JESUS

Sermon Title

Sermon Verse

Sermon Notes

What did you learn about Jesus today in church?

MEETING 20 | JESUS SHEPHERDS

We are about to meet Jesus as the shepherd of his sheep. No shepherd has ever loved his sheep like Jesus does. He leads them, protects them, dies for them, increases them, and holds them. As you meet Jesus this week, ask yourself if you are one of Jesus's sheep.

 TALKING TO JESUS: PRAYER POINTS

 REMEMBERING JESUS: MEMORY VERSE | JOHN 10:11

MONDAY | Jesus Leads His Sheep

 John 10:1–6

Answer:

 Why do Jesus's sheep follow him (v. 4)?

TUESDAY | Jesus Protects His Sheep

 John 10:7–10

Answer:

 Why did Jesus come (v. 10)?

WEDNESDAY | Jesus Dies for His Sheep

 John 10:11–16

Answer:

 What does the good shepherd give his sheep (v. 11)?

THURSDAY | Jesus Adds to His Sheep

 John 10:17–21

 Why does the Father love Jesus (v. 17)?

Answer:

FRIDAY | Jesus Identifies His Sheep

 John 10:22–27

 Describe Jesus's sheep (v. 27).

Answer:

SATURDAY | Jesus Holds His Sheep

 John 10:28–30

 Where does Jesus hold his sheep (v. 28)?

Answer:

SUNDAY | MEETING JESUS WITH OTHERS

 ## TALKING ABOUT JESUS

How do we know if we are one of Jesus's sheep (John 10:27)?

LISTENING TO JESUS

Sermon Title

Sermon Verse

Sermon Notes

What did you learn about Jesus today in church?

MEETING 21 | JESUS DEFEATS SATAN

We are now going to meet Jesus the harvester. The field is the world, the harvest is souls, and the harvester's helpers are his disciples. He sends out his workers into the harvest, tells them what to say and do, rejoices in their success, encourages love for neighbors, and calls his busy servants to rest at his feet.

 TALKING TO JESUS: PRAYER POINTS

 REMEMBERING JESUS: MEMORY VERSE | LUKE 10:2

MONDAY | Jesus Sends Out Missionaries

 Luke 10:1–8

Answer:

 What should we pray for (v. 2)?

TUESDAY | Jesus Gives His Message

 Luke 10:9–16

Answer:

 What had come near (v. 9, 11)?

WEDNESDAY | Jesus Rejoices in Satan's Defeat

 Luke 10:17–21

Answer:

 What did Jesus see when his disciples reported on their mission (v. 18)?

THURSDAY | Jesus Commands Love

 Luke 10:25–29

 What are we to love with (v. 27)?

Answer:

FRIDAY | Jesus Explains Love

 Luke 10:30–37

 What did Jesus say after he told the parable of the good Samaritan (v. 37)?

Answer:

SATURDAY | Jesus Stays with Martha and Mary

 Luke 10:38–42

 Martha was busy. Mary was sitting at Jesus's feet. Who did the right thing (v. 42)?

Answer:

SUNDAY | MEETING JESUS WITH OTHERS

 ## TALKING ABOUT JESUS

What missionaries do you pray for? Where do they serve the Lord? Why not write them a short letter to tell them that you pray for them, and ask them how their work is going.

 ## LISTENING TO JESUS

Sermon Title

Sermon Verse

Sermon Notes

What did you learn about Jesus today in church?

MEETING 22 | JESUS PROTECTS

A signpost directs us away from danger and to safety. This week we will meet Jesus as the greatest signpost, directing people to the safety of prayer, and away from the danger of the devil and darkness.

 TALKING TO JESUS: PRAYER POINTS

 REMEMBERING JESUS: MEMORY VERSE | LUKE 11:9

MONDAY | Jesus Teaches How to Keep Praying

 Luke 11:5–8

Answer:

 Why did the man eventually open the door (v. 8)?

TUESDAY | Jesus Teaches What to Pray For

 Luke 11:9–13

Answer:

 What should we pray for (v. 13)?

WEDNESDAY | Jesus Accused of Being the Devil

 Luke 11:14–23

Answer:

 How does Jesus cast out demons (v. 20)?

THURSDAY | Jesus Warns about the Devil

 Luke 11:24–28

 Who are blessed (v. 28)?

Answer:

FRIDAY | Jesus Is the Sign

 Luke 11:29–32

 Who is greater than Solomon or Jonah (v. 31, 32)?

Answer:

SATURDAY | Jesus Calls for Light

 Luke 11:33–36

 What is the lamp/light of your body (v. 34)?

Answer:

SUNDAY | MEETING JESUS WITH OTHERS

 ## TALKING ABOUT JESUS

In what ways was Jesus greater than Solomon (Luke 11:31) or Jonah (Luke 11:32)?

 ## LISTENING TO JESUS

Sermon Title

Sermon Verse

Sermon Notes

What did you learn about Jesus today in church?

MEETING 23 | JESUS JUDGES

A judge is someone who examines cases brought before him to decide if someone is innocent or guilty. If he finds them guilty, then he condemns them. That means he sentences them to judgment. This week we will meet Jesus as the judge who condemns the guilty to judgment.

 TALKING TO JESUS: PRAYER POINTS

 REMEMBERING JESUS: MEMORY VERSE | LUKE 12:5

MONDAY | Jesus Condemns Hypocrisy

 Luke 11:37–41

 What were the insides of the Pharisees like (v. 39)?

Answer:

TUESDAY | Jesus Condemns Disobedience

 Luke 11:42–44

 What did the Pharisees neglect/not do (v. 42)?

Answer:

WEDNESDAY | Jesus Condemns Cruelty

 Luke 11:45–51

 What did the lawyers or scribes do (v. 46)?

Answer:

THURSDAY | Jesus Condemns Bad Teachers

 Luke 11:52–54

 What did the lawyers take away (v. 52)?

Answer:

FRIDAY | Jesus Condemns Hidden Sins

 Luke 12:1–3

 What are we to beware of (v. 1)?

Answer:

SATURDAY | Jesus Condemns the Fear of People

 Luke 12:4–7

 Who are we to fear (v. 5)?

Answer:

SUNDAY | MEETING JESUS WITH OTHERS

 ## TALKING ABOUT JESUS

When we think of Jesus as judge, we realize that we must respect him (see your memory verse this week). How can you show your respect for Jesus?

LISTENING TO JESUS

Sermon Title

Sermon Verse

Sermon Notes

What did you learn about Jesus today in church?

MEETING 24 | JESUS WARNS

None of us like to be warned because it makes us afraid. However, when Jesus warned people, he did it out of love. This week we will meet Jesus giving the most loving warnings anyone has ever given.

 TALKING TO JESUS: PRAYER POINTS

 REMEMBERING JESUS: MEMORY VERSE | LUKE 12:31

MONDAY | Jesus Warns about Hiding Faith

 Luke 12:8–12

 What will happen if we confess Christ before others (v. 8)?

Answer:

TUESDAY | Jesus Warns about Greed

 Luke 12:13–15

Answer:

 What are we to be on guard about (v. 15)?

WEDNESDAY | Jesus Warns about Overconfidence

 Luke 12:16–21

Answer:

 What did God call the man who built bigger barns rather than get ready to die (v. 20)?

THURSDAY | Jesus Warns about Anxiety

 Luke 12:22–28

 What are we to look at to cure our worry (v. 24)?

Answer:

FRIDAY | Jesus Warns about Wrong Priorities

 Luke 12:29–31

 What should we seek before food, clothes, and everything else (v. 31)?

Answer:

SATURDAY | Jesus Warns about Money

 Luke 12:32–34

 What does God the Father love to do (v. 32)?

Answer:

SUNDAY | MEETING JESUS WITH OTHERS

 ## TALKING ABOUT JESUS

Jesus said that our heart will be where our treasure is (Luke 12:34). That means we will think most about what we value most. What do you think about most? What is your treasure?

 ## LISTENING TO JESUS

Sermon Title

Sermon Verse

Sermon Notes

What did you learn about Jesus today in church?

MEETING 25 | JESUS PREPARES

Although we cannot meet Jesus face-to-face now, he is coming back to this earth and we will all meet him face-to-face then. He wants us to be ready for that meeting. Let's listen to Jesus as he prepares us for his return.

 TALKING TO JESUS: PRAYER POINTS

 REMEMBERING JESUS: MEMORY VERSE | LUKE 12:40

MONDAY | Jesus Says, "Be Ready"

 Luke 12:35–40

Answer:

 When will Jesus return (v. 40)?

TUESDAY | Jesus Says, "Be Faithful"

 Luke 12:41–44

Answer:

 How will Jesus reward the faithful servant (v. 44)?

WEDNESDAY | Jesus Says, "Be Responsible"

 Luke 12:45–48

Answer:

 What happens to those who know God's will but don't do it (v. 47)?

THURSDAY | Jesus Says, "Be on Guard"

 Luke 12:49–53

 One result of Jesus's ministry
is d_____ (v. 51).

Answer:

FRIDAY | Jesus Says, "Be Watching"

 Luke 12:54–56

 What does Jesus call some
of his hearers (v. 56)?

Answer:

SATURDAY | Jesus Says, "Be Reconciled"

 Luke 12:57–59

 Fighting with people can
result in us standing before
the j_____ (v. 58).

Answer:

 SUNDAY | MEETING JESUS WITH OTHERS

 TALKING ABOUT JESUS

What are you doing to get ready for Jesus's return?

 **LISTENING TO JESUS**

Sermon Title

Sermon Verse

Sermon Notes

What did you learn about Jesus today in church?

MEETING 26 | JESUS ILLUSTRATES

Jesus was the best teacher ever. One of the reasons he was such a good teacher was that he taught deep truths in a simple way. He illustrated his teaching by drawing lessons from two tragedies; by telling the stories of a barren fig tree, of farmers and their animals, and of door-knocking; by comparing Herod to a fox; and by comparing himself to a mother hen.

 TALKING TO JESUS: PRAYER POINTS

 REMEMBERING JESUS: MEMORY VERSE | LUKE 13:24

MONDAY | Jesus Calls to Repentance

 Luke 13:1–5

Answer:

 What must we do if we do not want to perish (v. 5)?

TUESDAY | Jesus Looks for Fruit

 Luke 13:6–9

Answer:

 What happens to trees that don't produce fruit (v. 9)?

WEDNESDAY | Jesus Heals a Disabled Woman

 Luke 13:10–17

Answer:

 What did the woman do when Jesus healed her (v. 13)?

THURSDAY | Jesus Guards the Door

 Luke 13:22–30

 Who will be seen in the kingdom of God (v. 28)?

Answer:

FRIDAY | Jesus Stands Up to Herod

 Luke 13:31–35

 What did Jesus call Herod (v. 32)?

Answer:

SATURDAY | Jesus Appeals to Jerusalem

 Luke 13:34–35

 What did Jerusalem do to the prophets (v. 34)?

Answer:

SUNDAY | MEETING JESUS WITH OTHERS

 ## TALKING ABOUT JESUS

Jesus taught spiritual truths using tragic current events and by illustrating spiritual truths with trees, doors, foxes, and hens. Can you remember any other illustrations that Jesus used to teach us deep truths in a simple way?

LISTENING TO JESUS

Sermon Title

Sermon Verse

Sermon Notes

What did you learn about Jesus today in church?

MEETING 27 | JESUS CHANGES

Many men have tried to change the world by violence. Jesus changes the world by teaching. He turned people's thoughts upside down. This week we meet Jesus changing people's views about the Sabbath, about the high and the low, about who should be invited to dinner, and about who should come first in our lives.

TALKING TO JESUS: PRAYER POINTS

REMEMBERING JESUS: MEMORY VERSE | LUKE 14:11

MONDAY | Jesus Does Good on the Sabbath

 Luke 14:1–6

Answer:

 How did the Pharisees answer Jesus (v. 6)?

TUESDAY | Jesus Lifts Up the Humble

 Luke 14:7–11

Answer:

 What happens to those who exalt themselves (v. 11)?

WEDNESDAY | Jesus Invites the Poor

 Luke 14:12–14

Answer:

 Who should we call to eat with us (v. 13)?

THURSDAY | Jesus Exposes Excuses

 Luke 14:15–24

 What did the servant say to those invited to the supper (v. 17)?

Answer:

FRIDAY | Jesus Offers a Cross

 Luke 14:25–30

 What does the man do before he builds a tower (v. 28)?

Answer:

SATURDAY | Jesus Counts the Cost

 Luke 14:31–35

 Who cannot be Jesus's disciple (v. 33)?

Answer:

 # SUNDAY | MEETING JESUS WITH OTHERS

 ## TALKING ABOUT JESUS

What sin do you need to leave behind to follow Jesus in your life (Luke 14:33)?

 ## LISTENING TO JESUS

Sermon Title

Sermon Verse

Sermon Notes

What did you learn about Jesus today in church?

MEETING 28 | JESUS FINDS

We've all lost lots of things in our lives. We searched high and low but without success. When Jesus searches for lost sinners, he always finds them. Meet Jesus, the finder of the lost.

 TALKING TO JESUS: PRAYER POINTS

 REMEMBERING JESUS: MEMORY VERSE | LUKE 15:10

MONDAY | Jesus Rejoices over Finding a Lost Sheep

 Luke 15:1–7

Answer:

 What does the Shepherd say when he returns home with his lost sheep (v. 6)?

TUESDAY | Jesus Rejoices over Finding a Lost Coin

 Luke 15:8–10

Answer:

 What happens when a sinner repents (v. 10)?

WEDNESDAY | Jesus Describes a Sinful Life

 Luke 15:11–16

Answer:

 What did the son do in the faraway country (v. 13)?

THURSDAY | Jesus Marks a Turning Point

 Luke 15:17–19

 What did the son plan to say to his father (v. 18)?

Answer:

FRIDAY | Jesus Welcomes Sinners

 Luke 15:20–24

 What did the father say about his son (v. 24)?

Answer:

SATURDAY | Jesus Warns against Pride

 Luke 15:25–32

 What was the right thing to do when the son returned home (v. 32)?

Answer:

SUNDAY | MEETING JESUS WITH OTHERS

 ## TALKING ABOUT JESUS

What feeling does Jesus have when he saves sinners like us (Luke 15:5, 6, 9, 32)?

 ## LISTENING TO JESUS

Sermon Title

Sermon Verse

Sermon Notes

What did you learn about Jesus today in church?

MEETING 29 | JESUS STEWARDS

A steward is someone who manages money and property for someone else. Because money can cause us lots of spiritual problems, Jesus teaches us how to handle it and manage it so that it helps us rather than harms us.

 TALKING TO JESUS: PRAYER POINTS

 REMEMBERING JESUS: MEMORY VERSE | LUKE 16:13

MONDAY | Jesus Condemns Wasting Money

 Luke 16:1–4

Answer:

 What was the manager (steward) accused of (v. 1)?

TUESDAY | Jesus Commends Wisdom with Money

 Luke 16:5–9

Answer:

 What did the master do to the dishonest manager (v. 8)?

WEDNESDAY | Jesus Puts God above Money

 Luke 16:10–13

Answer:

 How many masters can we serve (v. 13)?

THURSDAY | Jesus Puts God above People

 Luke 16:14–18

 What does God know (v. 15)?

Answer:

FRIDAY | Jesus Warns about the Rich Man in Hell

 Luke 16:19–26

 Where did the rich man go after he died (v. 23)?

Answer:

SATURDAY | Jesus Calls to Faith in the Bible

 Luke 16:27–31

 Would more believe in Jesus if someone came back from the dead (v. 31)?

Answer:

SUNDAY | MEETING JESUS WITH OTHERS

 ## TALKING ABOUT JESUS

What did you learn about money this week?

 ## LISTENING TO JESUS

Sermon Title

Sermon Verse

Sermon Notes

What did you learn about Jesus today in church?

MEETING 30 | JESUS RESURRECTS

One of Jesus's best friends was a man called Lazarus who lived in Bethany. This week we will see what Jesus says and does when he hears that his dear friend has died.

 TALKING TO JESUS: PRAYER POINTS

 REMEMBERING JESUS: MEMORY VERSE | JOHN 11:25

MONDAY | Jesus's Friend Is Sick

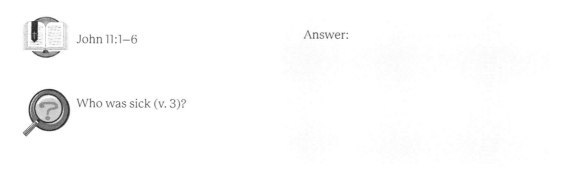

John 11:1–6

Answer:

Who was sick (v. 3)?

TUESDAY | Jesus's Friend Is Dead

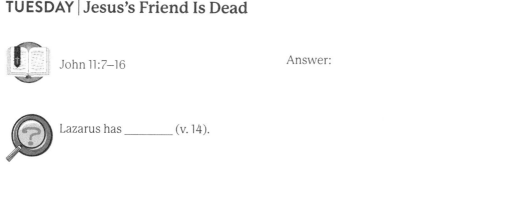

John 11:7–16

Answer:

Lazarus has _____ (v. 14).

WEDNESDAY | Jesus Is the Resurrection and the Life

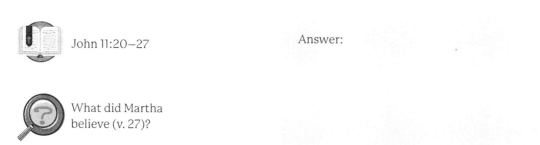

John 11:20–27

Answer:

What did Martha believe (v. 27)?

THURSDAY | Jesus Weeps with His Friends

 John 11:32–37

 Jesus _____ (v. 35).

Answer:

FRIDAY | Jesus Removes the Stone

 John 11:38–40

 If we believe, we will see the g_____ of G___ (v. 40).

Answer:

SATURDAY | Jesus Raises the Dead

 John 11:41–44

 Describe Lazarus as he came out of the tomb (v. 44).

Answer:

SUNDAY | MEETING JESUS WITH OTHERS

 ## TALKING ABOUT JESUS

Think about your memory verse for this week (John 11:25). What does Jesus mean when he says, "I am the resurrection"?

 ## LISTENING TO JESUS

Sermon Title

Sermon Verse

Sermon Notes

What did you learn about Jesus today in church?

MEETING 31 | JESUS REIGNS

As King of kings, Jesus protects the little ones in his kingdom and calls his servants to serve him. He reigns over leprosy, and he heals, even though only one healed leper returns to thank him. At the moment, Jesus's kingdom is mainly in people's hearts, but when he returns, his kingdom will cover the whole earth and he will cast out all rebels.

 TALKING TO JESUS: PRAYER POINTS

 REMEMBERING JESUS: MEMORY VERSE | LUKE 17:10

MONDAY | Jesus Protects His Little Ones

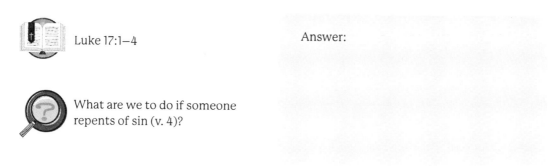

Luke 17:1–4

Answer:

What are we to do if someone repents of sin (v. 4)?

TUESDAY | Jesus on Faith and Faithfulness

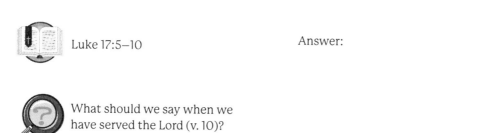

Luke 17:5–10

Answer:

What should we say when we have served the Lord (v. 10)?

WEDNESDAY | Jesus Heals Even the Ungrateful

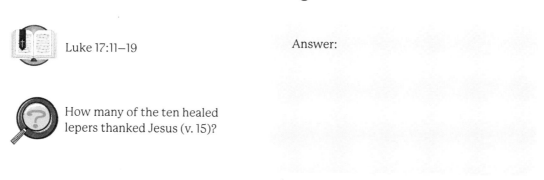

Luke 17:11–19

Answer:

How many of the ten healed lepers thanked Jesus (v. 15)?

THURSDAY | Jesus Is Coming Back

 Luke 17:20–25

 Where is the kingdom of heaven (v. 21)?

Answer:

FRIDAY | Jesus Prepares for the End

 Luke 17:26–30

 What happened when Lot left Sodom (v. 29)?

Answer:

SATURDAY | Jesus Warns the Unprepared

 Luke 17:31–37

 Who are we to remember (v. 32)?

Answer:

SUNDAY | MEETING JESUS WITH OTHERS

 ## TALKING ABOUT JESUS

If Jesus is King, then we are his servants. How will you serve King Jesus this week?

 ## LISTENING TO JESUS

Sermon Title

Sermon Verse

Sermon Notes

What did you learn about Jesus today in church?

MEETING 32 | JESUS BEFRIENDS

Jesus had a special place in his heart for children. He loved to be their friend. This week we meet him encouraging children to come to him, using children to illustrate receiving the kingdom of God, and protecting children by strengthening marriage.

 TALKING TO JESUS: PRAYER POINTS

 REMEMBERING JESUS: MEMORY VERSE | LUKE 18:16

MONDAY | Jesus Teaches Us to Pray

 Luke 18:1–8

Answer:

 What should we always be doing (v. 1)?

TUESDAY | Jesus on Humility

 Luke 18:9–14

Answer:

 What did the publican or tax collector pray (v. 13)?

WEDNESDAY | Jesus Strengthens Marriage

 Matthew 19:1–6

Answer:

 What God has joined together _____ (v. 6).

THURSDAY | Jesus Encourages Children

 Luke 18:15–17

 We are to receive the kingdom of God like_____ (v. 17).

Answer:

FRIDAY | Jesus Calls a Rich Ruler

 Luke 18:18–23

 Why did the ruler not want to follow Jesus (v. 23)?

Answer:

SATURDAY | Jesus Predicts His Death and Resurrection

 Luke 18:31–34

 What will happen to Jesus in Jerusalem (v. 33)?

Answer:

SUNDAY | MEETING JESUS WITH OTHERS

TALKING ABOUT JESUS

Jesus welcomed little children (Luke 18:16). What does that tell you about Jesus?

LISTENING TO JESUS

Sermon Title

Sermon Verse

Sermon Notes

What did you learn about Jesus today in church?

MEETING 33 | JESUS GIFTS

This week we meet Jesus giving sight to the blind, giving a generous heart to a greedy man, and giving talents to everyone. We will also discover the importance of how we use the good gifts Jesus gives us.

 TALKING TO JESUS: PRAYER POINTS

 REMEMBERING JESUS: MEMORY VERSE | LUKE 19:10

MONDAY | Jesus Gives Sight to the Blind

 Luke 18:35–43

 What did the blind man pray (v. 38)?

Answer:

TUESDAY | Jesus Calls Zacchaeus

 Luke 19:1–6

 What did Zacchaeus do when Jesus called him (v. 6)?

Answer:

WEDNESDAY | Jesus Gives Zacchaeus a Generous Heart

 Luke 19:7–10

 Who did Jesus come to save (v. 10)?

Answer:

THURSDAY | Jesus Gives Talents

Luke 19:11–14

What did the people say
to the nobleman (v. 14)?

Answer:

FRIDAY | Jesus Rewards Good Use of Talents

Luke 19:15–19

What did the nobleman
say to the servant (v. 17)?

Answer:

SATURDAY | Jesus Punishes Misuse of Talents

Luke 19:20–27

What will happen to
rebels who reject the
nobleman's reign (v. 27)?

Answer:

SUNDAY | MEETING JESUS WITH OTHERS

 ## TALKING ABOUT JESUS

What talents (gifts) has the Master given you and how are you using them for him?

 ## LISTENING TO JESUS

Sermon Title

Sermon Verse

Sermon Notes

What did you learn about Jesus today in church?

MEETING 34 | JESUS WEEPS

This week we meet Jesus in a rare moment of triumph. He enters Jerusalem with multitudes praising him as the King who brings peace to people and glory to God. Yet, he knew this praise would not last and wept because the very people who praised him would soon oppose him and even call for his death.

TALKING TO JESUS: PRAYER POINTS

REMEMBERING JESUS: MEMORY VERSE | LUKE 19:38

MONDAY | Jesus Arranges Transport into Jerusalem

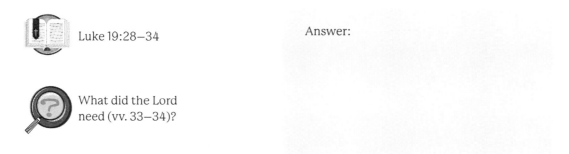

Luke 19:28–34

What did the Lord
need (vv. 33–34)?

Answer:

TUESDAY | Jesus Enters Jerusalem

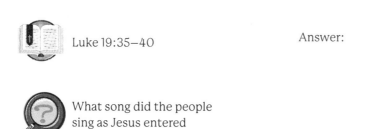

Luke 19:35–40

What song did the people
sing as Jesus entered
Jerusalem (v. 38)?

Answer:

WEDNESDAY | Jesus Weeps over Jerusalem

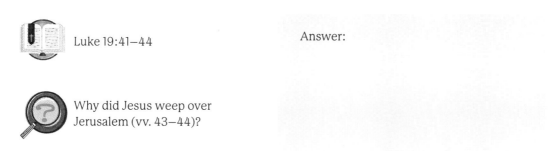

Luke 19:41–44

Why did Jesus weep over
Jerusalem (vv. 43–44)?

Answer:

THURSDAY | Jesus Cleanses Jerusalem

 Luke 19:45–48

 What did Jesus call the temple (v. 46)?

Answer:

FRIDAY | Jesus Challenged in Jerusalem

 Luke 20:1–4

 What did Jesus do in the temple (v. 1)?

Answer:

SATURDAY | Jesus Silences His Opponents

 Luke 20:5–8

 What did Jesus answer his critics (v. 8)?

Answer:

SUNDAY | MEETING JESUS WITH OTHERS

 ## TALKING ABOUT JESUS

Jesus wept over the death of Lazarus (John 11:35) and the unbelief in Jerusalem (Luke 19:41). How does this help you to draw near to Jesus? (Heb. 4:15; 5:2).

 ## LISTENING TO JESUS

Sermon Title

Sermon Verse

Sermon Notes

What did you learn about Jesus today in church?

MEETING 35 | JESUS OPPOSED

Though Jesus was praised when he entered Jerusalem, there soon was growing opposition to his teaching. But he did not give up, give in, or run away. He was like an immoveable cornerstone of a building that would not move no matter how much it was attacked. Let's meet Jesus as he bravely responds to his opponents.

 TALKING TO JESUS: PRAYER POINTS

 REMEMBERING JESUS: MEMORY VERSE | LUKE 20:17

MONDAY | Jesus Will Be Killed by His Opponents

 Luke 20:9–13

Answer:

 When the vinedressers killed the servants, what did the owner do (v. 13)?

TUESDAY | Jesus Will Judge His Opponents

 Luke 20:14–19

Answer:

 What will happen to the stone that the builders rejected (v. 17)?

WEDNESDAY | Jesus Hated by His Opponents

 Luke 20:20–26

Answer:

 What did Jesus say about Caesar (v. 25)?

THURSDAY | Jesus Questioned by His Opponents

 Luke 20:27–33

 What did the Sadducees not believe or deny (v. 27)?

Answer:

FRIDAY | Jesus Silences His Opponents

 Luke 20:34–40

 God is not the God of the d_____ but of the l_____ (v. 38).

Answer:

SATURDAY | Jesus Questions His Opponents

 Luke 20:41–47

 What will happen to the Lord's enemies (v. 43)?

Answer:

SUNDAY | MEETING JESUS WITH OTHERS

 ## TALKING ABOUT JESUS

In what ways is Jesus like a cornerstone of a building? (Luke 20:17–18) Is he the cornerstone of your life?

 ## LISTENING TO JESUS

Sermon Title

Sermon Verse

Sermon Notes

What did you learn about Jesus today in church?

MEETING 36 | JESUS APPROVES

Although Jesus was cast down at the opposition to him, in this meeting we meet Jesus lifted up in his spirit by the news of the Greeks who wanted to know him. But he then predicts that he is to be lifted up in another way—that is, on the cross. We also see God approving his Son, and the Son approving a woman's giving heart.

 TALKING TO JESUS: PRAYER POINTS

 REMEMBERING JESUS: MEMORY VERSE | JOHN 12:32

MONDAY | Jesus Sought by Greeks

 John 12:20–26

Answer:

 What did the Greeks say (v. 21)?

TUESDAY | Jesus Approved by his Father

 John 12:27–30

Answer:

 What did Jesus pray (v. 28)?

WEDNESDAY | Jesus Predicts His Lifting Up

 John 12:31–36

Answer:

 What will happen when Jesus is lifted up (v. 32)?

THURSDAY | Jesus Fulfills Prophecy

 John 12:37–43

 Why did some Pharisees not confess Jesus (v. 43)?

Answer:

FRIDAY | Jesus Speaks God's Words

 John 12:44–50

 John 12:45

Write the verse:

SATURDAY | Jesus on Generous Giving

 Luke 21:1–4

 Who put the most into the collection (v. 3)?

Answer:

SUNDAY | MEETING JESUS WITH OTHERS

 ## TALKING ABOUT JESUS

Every prediction that Jesus made about the end of his life came true. What should this teach us about Jesus's predictions about the end of the world?

 ## LISTENING TO JESUS

Sermon Title

Sermon Verse

Sermon Notes

What did you learn about Jesus today in church?

MEETING 37 | JESUS FINISHES

Jesus will bring everything to an end. There will be signs before the end, such as the persecution of God's people. But Jesus will keep his word and come back to rescue his people and punish their enemies.

 TALKING TO JESUS: PRAYER POINTS

 REMEMBERING JESUS: MEMORY VERSE | LUKE 21:33

MONDAY | Jesus on the Signs of the End

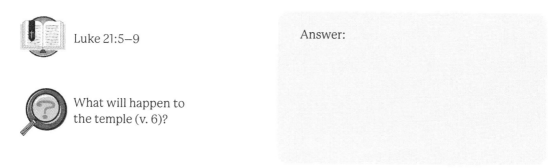

Luke 21:5–9

What will happen to the temple (v. 6)?

Answer:

TUESDAY | Jesus's Followers Will Suffer

Luke 21:10–19

What does Jesus promise his suffering people (v. 18)?

Answer:

WEDNESDAY | Jesus on the Destruction of Jerusalem

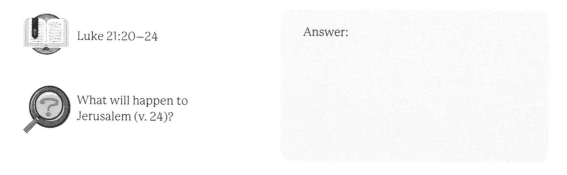

Luke 21:20–24

What will happen to Jerusalem (v. 24)?

Answer:

THURSDAY | Jesus Will Come in Glory

 Luke 21:25–28

 How will Jesus come (v. 27)?

Answer:

FRIDAY | Jesus's Words Will Endure

 Luke 21:29–33

 What will happen to God's Word (v. 33)?

Answer:

SATURDAY | Jesus Calls Us to Watch

 Luke 21:34–38

 What does Jesus urge his followers to do (v. 36)?

Answer:

SUNDAY | MEETING JESUS WITH OTHERS

 ## TALKING ABOUT JESUS

Jesus said that because he is coming to end everything, we are to watch and pray (Luke 21:36). What does that mean?

 ## LISTENING TO JESUS

Sermon Title

Sermon Verse

Sermon Notes

What did you learn about Jesus today in church?

MEETING 38 | JESUS SUBSTITUTES

A substitute is someone who takes the place of another. Jesus came to this world as a substitute, to take the place of sinners, to be punished in their place. This truth is taught by Jesus when he sits down to eat the Passover with his disciples and changes it into the Lord's Supper. Both the Passover and the Lord's Supper point to the death of one that gives life to others.

 TALKING TO JESUS: PRAYER POINTS

 REMEMBERING JESUS: MEMORY VERSE | LUKE 22:19

MONDAY | Jesus Anointed for Burial

 John 12:1–3

Answer:

 What did Mary do (v. 3)?

TUESDAY | Jesus Defends His Anointer

 John 12:4–8

Answer:

 What did Jesus say about the poor (v. 8)?

WEDNESDAY | Jesus Is Betrayed

 Luke 22:1–6

Answer:

 Who entered into Judas (v. 3)?

THURSDAY | Jesus Prepares the Passover

 Luke 22:7–13

 Where did Jesus and the disciples eat the Passover (v. 12)?

Answer:

FRIDAY | Jesus Eats the Passover

 Luke 22:14–16

 Luke 22:15

Write the verse:

SATURDAY | Jesus Institutes the Lord's Supper

 Luke 22:17–23

 What did the bread point to (v. 19)?

Answer:

SUNDAY | MEETING JESUS WITH OTHERS

 ## TALKING ABOUT JESUS

Jesus gave the church the Lord's Supper to remind us of his death (Luke 22:19). Why is remembering his death so important?

 ## LISTENING TO JESUS

Sermon Title

Sermon Verse

Sermon Notes

What did you learn about Jesus today in church?

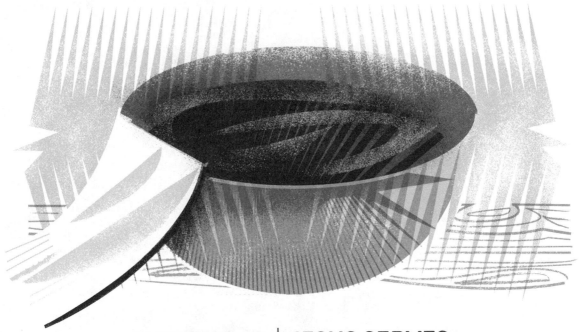

MEETING 39 | JESUS SERVES

Although Jesus was Lord of all, he became the servant of his disciples. This week we meet him on the floor with a towel and a basin as he washes his disciples' feet.

 TALKING TO JESUS: PRAYER POINTS

 REMEMBERING JESUS: MEMORY VERSE | JOHN 13:34

MONDAY | Jesus Loves His Disciples

 John 13:1–5

Answer:

 Why did Jesus wash his disciples' feet (v. 1)?

TUESDAY | Jesus Washes His Disciples' Feet

 John 13:6–11

Answer:

 What did Jesus already know (v. 11)?

WEDNESDAY | Jesus Commends Feet Washing

 John 13:12–17

Answer:

 What should we do (v. 14)?

THURSDAY | Jesus Gets Ready to Suffer

 John 13:18–22

 Why did Jesus predict the future (v. 19)?

Answer:

FRIDAY | Jesus Identifies His Betrayer

 John 13:23–30

 Who entered Judas (v. 27)?

Answer:

SATURDAY | Jesus Issues a New Commandment

 John 13:31–35

 How will people know Christ's disciples (v. 35)?

Answer:

SUNDAY | MEETING JESUS WITH OTHERS

 ## TALKING ABOUT JESUS

How do you show that you are one of Jesus's disciples (John 13:35)?

 ## LISTENING TO JESUS

Sermon Title

Sermon Verse

Sermon Notes

What did you learn about Jesus today in church?

MEETING 40 | JESUS CALMS

Although Jesus is about to suffer terrible violence, he wants his disciples to have peace. He helps them to find peace by assuring them of their place in heaven, by showing them who God really is, by promising them the comfort of the Holy Spirit, and by living in their hearts.

 TALKING TO JESUS: PRAYER POINTS

 REMEMBERING JESUS: MEMORY VERSE | JOHN 14:6

MONDAY | Jesus Warns His Disciples

 John 13:36–38

Answer:

 What did Jesus predict (v. 38)?

TUESDAY | Jesus Is the Way, Truth, and Life

 John 14:1–6

Answer:

 How do we get to God the Father (v. 6)?

WEDNESDAY | Jesus Shows Us the Father

 John 14:7–11

Answer:

 He who has seen Jesus has seen the F_____ (v. 9).

THURSDAY | Jesus Promises the Holy Spirit

 John 14:12–18

 What does Jesus pray for (vv. 16–17)?

Answer:

FRIDAY | Jesus Lives in His People

 John 14:19–24

 What will Jesus do for those who love him (v. 23)?

Answer:

SATURDAY | Jesus Gives Peace

 John 14:25–31

 What does Jesus leave with his people (v. 27)?

Answer:

SUNDAY | MEETING JESUS WITH OTHERS

 ## TALKING ABOUT JESUS

How have you known Christ's peace in the middle of trouble? Ask some other Christians how they have known Christ's peace when they have been troubled.

 ## LISTENING TO JESUS

Sermon Title

Sermon Verse

Sermon Notes

What did you learn about Jesus today in church?

MEETING 41 | JESUS MAKES FRUITFUL

Now we meet Jesus as the true vine, the one who gives both fruitfulness and joy.

TALKING TO JESUS: PRAYER POINTS

REMEMBERING JESUS: MEMORY VERSE | JOHN 15:5

MONDAY | Jesus Is the True Vine

 John 15:1–4

Answer:

 How do you bear fruit (v. 4)?

TUESDAY | Jesus Makes Us Fruitful

 John 15:5–8

Answer:

 What can you do without Jesus (v. 5)?

WEDNESDAY | Jesus Gives Joy

 John 15:9–11

Answer:

 Why did Jesus speak these things (v. 11)?

THURSDAY | Jesus Gives His Life

 John 15:12–17

 What is the greatest proof of love (v. 13)?

Answer:

FRIDAY | Jesus Is Not of This World

 John 15:18–21

 Why do some people hate Christians (v. 19)?

Answer:

SATURDAY | Jesus Is Hated

 John 15:22–27

 Why do people hate Jesus (v. 25)?

Answer:

SUNDAY | MEETING JESUS WITH OTHERS

 ## TALKING ABOUT JESUS

Jesus calls his people to bear much fruit (Luke 15:8). What kind of fruit can be seen in your life?

 ## LISTENING TO JESUS

Sermon Title

Sermon Verse

Sermon Notes

What did you learn about Jesus today in church?

MEETING 42 | JESUS COMFORTS

Jesus is about to leave this world. His disciples are very sad. But he cheers them up by promising them that when he leaves, he will send the Holy Spirit, who will be with all believers all the time.

 TALKING TO JESUS: PRAYER POINTS

 REMEMBERING JESUS: MEMORY VERSE | JOHN 16:33
(Start with "In the world")

MONDAY | Jesus Prepares His Disciples

 John 16:1–6

Answer:

 What were Jesus's disciples feeling (v. 6)?

TUESDAY | Jesus Sends the Holy Spirit

 John 16:7–11

Answer:

 Who will Jesus send in his place (v. 7)?

WEDNESDAY | Jesus Is Glorified by the Holy Spirit

 John 16:12–15

Answer:

 What will the Holy Spirit do (v. 14)?

THURSDAY | Jesus Leaves for a Little While

 John 16:16–22

 What will happen to the disciples' sorrow (v. 22)?

Answer:

FRIDAY | Jesus Goes to His Father

 John 16:23–28

 Where is Jesus going (v. 28)?

Answer:

SATURDAY | Jesus Overcomes the World

 John 16:29–33

 What will we experience in this world (v. 33)?

Answer:

SUNDAY | MEETING JESUS WITH OTHERS

 ## TALKING ABOUT JESUS

The Holy Spirit comforts the hearts of believers. What does he do for unbelievers (John 16:8–9)?

 ## LISTENING TO JESUS

Sermon Title

Sermon Verse

Sermon Notes

What did you learn about Jesus today in church?

MEETING 43 | JESUS PRAYS

A priest offers sacrifice and prays for people. Soon we shall see Jesus offering his sacrifice, but in this meeting he is praying for his people. It is the most beautiful prayer in the world.

 TALKING TO JESUS: PRAYER POINTS

 REMEMBERING JESUS: MEMORY VERSE | JOHN 17:3

MONDAY | Jesus Prays for Restored Glory

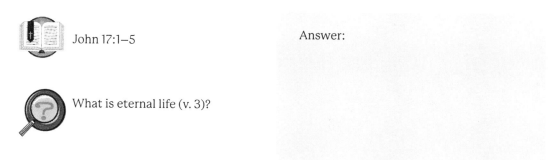

John 17:1–5

What is eternal life (v. 3)?

Answer:

TUESDAY | Jesus Prays for His People

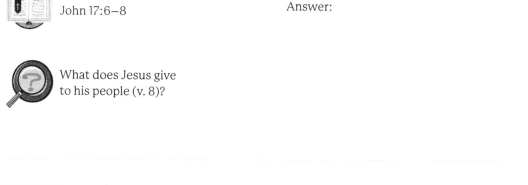

John 17:6–8

What does Jesus give
to his people (v. 8)?

Answer:

WEDNESDAY | Jesus Prays for His People's Protection

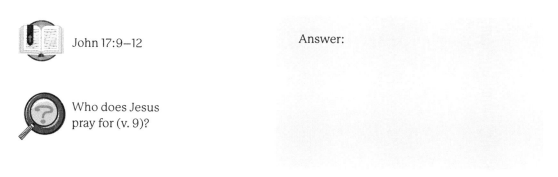

John 17:9–12

Who does Jesus
pray for (v. 9)?

Answer:

THURSDAY | Jesus Prays for His People's Holiness

 John 17:13–19

 Why did Jesus speak these words (v. 13)?

Answer:

FRIDAY | Jesus Prays for His People's Unity

 John 17:20–23

 What does Jesus want the world to know (v. 23)?

Answer:

SATURDAY | Jesus Prays for His People's Company

 John 17:24–26

 What did Jesus want (v. 24)?

Answer:

SUNDAY | MEETING JESUS WITH OTHERS

 ## TALKING ABOUT JESUS

This week we studied Jesus's prayer. What did you learn about what you should pray for?

 ## LISTENING TO JESUS

Sermon Title

Sermon Verse

Sermon Notes

What did you learn about Jesus today in church?

MEETING 44 | JESUS DESERTED

Though Jesus was the best of friends, his friends all let him down him at his lowest point. This week we will see Jesus's disciples sleeping instead of praying for him, Judas betraying him, and Peter denying him.

 TALKING TO JESUS: PRAYER POINTS

 REMEMBERING JESUS: MEMORY VERSE | LUKE 22:42

MONDAY | Jesus Prepares His Disciples

 Luke 22:35–38

Answer:

 Who will Jesus be numbered with (v. 37)?

TUESDAY | Jesus Prays in Gethsemane

 Luke 22:39–44

Answer:

 What did Jesus pray (v. 42)?

WEDNESDAY | Jesus Betrayed with a Kiss

 Luke 22:45–48

Answer:

 What did Jesus ask Judas (v. 48)?

THURSDAY | Jesus Heals His Enemy

 Luke 22:49–53

 How did Jesus's enemies treat him (v. 52)?

Answer:

FRIDAY | Jesus Denied by Peter

 Luke 22:54–57

 What did Peter reply to the young woman (v. 57)?

Answer:

SATURDAY | Jesus Looks at Peter

 Luke 22:58–62

 What did Peter do when he remembered Jesus's words (v. 62)?

Answer:

SUNDAY | MEETING JESUS WITH OTHERS

 ## TALKING ABOUT JESUS

Contrast the way Jesus's disciples deserted him with Jesus's promise to his people in Hebrews 13:5. What does this tell you about yourself? What does this tell you about Jesus?

 ## LISTENING TO JESUS

Sermon Title

Sermon Verse

Sermon Notes

What did you learn about Jesus today in church?

MEETING 45 | JESUS IS JUDGED

Although Jesus is the judge of everyone, he allowed himself to be judged in the place of sinners so that they could go free. Here we meet Jesus being judged by the Jewish church, the Jewish court, Herod, and Pilate.

 TALKING TO JESUS: PRAYER POINTS

 REMEMBERING JESUS: MEMORY VERSE | LUKE 23:4

MONDAY | Jesus Tried by the Jewish Church

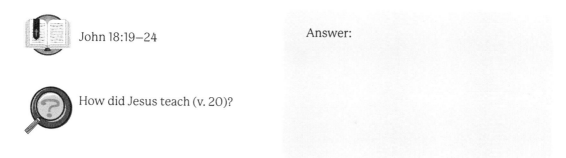

John 18:19–24

How did Jesus teach (v. 20)?

Answer:

TUESDAY | Jesus Tried by the Jewish Court

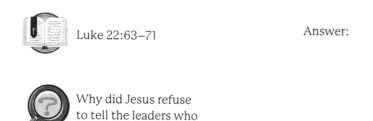

Luke 22:63–71

Why did Jesus refuse to tell the leaders who he was (v. 67)?

Answer:

WEDNESDAY | Jesus Tried by Pilate

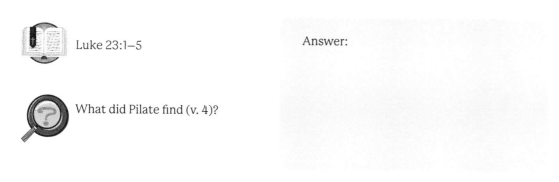

Luke 23:1–5

What did Pilate find (v. 4)?

Answer:

THURSDAY | Jesus Tried by Herod

 Luke 23:6–12

 What did Jesus answer Herod (v. 9)?

Answer:

FRIDAY | Jesus Cleared by Pilate

 Luke 23:13–17

 What did Pilate want to do (v. 16)?

Answer:

SATURDAY | Jesus Condemned by Pilate

 Luke 23:18–25

 Who did Pilate release instead of Jesus (v. 18, 25)?

Answer:

SUNDAY | MEETING JESUS WITH OTHERS

 ## TALKING ABOUT JESUS

Innocent Jesus was condemned but the murderer Barabbas was released. How is this a picture of the gospel?

 ## LISTENING TO JESUS

Sermon Title

Sermon Verse

Sermon Notes

What did you learn about Jesus today in church?

MEETING 46 | JESUS DIES

Although Jesus had suffered throughout his life, his sufferings came to a climax at the cross. And yet even there, as he offered his life as a sacrifice to God, he was able to comfort his people, pray for his enemies, save a thief, and trust his Father.

 TALKING TO JESUS: PRAYER POINTS

 REMEMBERING JESUS: MEMORY VERSE | LUKE 23:43

MONDAY | Jesus Comforts Women

 Luke 23:26–31

Answer:

 What did Jesus say to the weeping women (v. 28)?

TUESDAY | Jesus Forgives His Enemies

 Luke 23:32–38

Answer:

 What did Jesus pray for his enemies (v. 34)?

WEDNESDAY | Jesus Saves a Criminal

 Luke 23:39–43

Answer:

 What did the dying thief pray (v. 42)?

THURSDAY | Jesus Trusts His Father

 Luke 23:44–46

 What was Jesus's last prayer (v. 46)?

Answer:

FRIDAY | Jesus Impresses a Centurion

 Luke 23:47–49

 What did the centurion say when Jesus died (v. 47)?

Answer:

SATURDAY | Jesus Buried in a Borrowed Tomb

 Luke 23:50–56

 What did Joseph ask Pilate for (v. 52)?

Answer:

SUNDAY | MEETING JESUS WITH OTHERS

 ## TALKING ABOUT JESUS

Jesus's sufferings are not just sad. They are also saving. What did Jesus offer to save us from sin? See Hebrews 10:12 and 1 Peter 1:18–19.

LISTENING TO JESUS

Sermon Title

Sermon Verse

Sermon Notes

What did you learn about Jesus today in church?

MEETING 47 | JESUS LIVES

This Sunday morning meeting in the garden with the resurrected Jesus must have been the happiest meeting ever. He is risen from the dead!

 TALKING TO JESUS: PRAYER POINTS

 REMEMBERING JESUS: MEMORY VERSE | JOHN 20:29

MONDAY | Jesus Rises from the Dead

 John 20:1–5

Answer:

 When did Mary go to Jesus's tomb (v. 1)?

TUESDAY | Jesus Surprises the Disciples

 John 20:6–10

Answer:

 What did the disciples not know (v. 9)?

WEDNESDAY | Jesus Talks to Mary

 John 20:11–14

Answer:

 Why was Mary weeping (v. 13)?

THURSDAY | Jesus Reveals Himself to Mary

 John 20:15–18

 What did Mary tell the disciples (v. 18)?

Answer:

FRIDAY | Jesus Appears to His disciples

 John 20:19–23

 What were Jesus's first words to his disciples (v. 19)?

Answer:

SATURDAY | Jesus Appears to Thomas

 John 20:24–29

 Who are most blessed (v. 29)?

Answer:

SUNDAY | MEETING JESUS WITH OTHERS

 ## TALKING ABOUT JESUS

The disciples were so happy when they saw the Lord, especially when they saw the scars on his hands and his side. Why did these scars make them so happy?

LISTENING TO JESUS

Sermon Title

Sermon Verse

Sermon Notes

What did you learn about Jesus today in church?

MEETING 48 | JESUS WARMS HEARTS

Have you ever enjoyed talking to someone so much that you felt a warm feeling in your heart? That's what two disciples are about to experience as a result of an unexpected meeting with Jesus.

 TALKING TO JESUS: PRAYER POINTS

 REMEMBERING JESUS: MEMORY VERSE | LUKE 24:32

MONDAY | Jesus Walks with Two Disciples

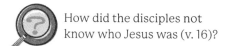 Luke 24:13–16

Answer:

How did the disciples not know who Jesus was (v. 16)?

TUESDAY | Jesus Questions the Two Disciples

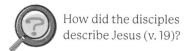 Luke 24:17–20

Answer:

How did the disciples describe Jesus (v. 19)?

WEDNESDAY | Jesus Listens to the Two Disciples

Luke 24:21–24

Answer:

What had the disciples hoped for (v. 21)?

THURSDAY | Jesus Opens the Eyes of the Two Disciples

 Luke 24:25–31

 Where did Jesus preach from to the disciples (v. 27)?

Answer:

FRIDAY | Jesus Warms the Hearts of the Two Disciples

 Luke 24:32–35

 What happened to the two disciples' hearts as they listened to Jesus (v. 32)?

Answer:

SATURDAY | Jesus Reported Missing

 Matthew 28:11–15

 What lie were the soldiers paid to tell (vv. 12–13)?

Answer:

SUNDAY | MEETING JESUS WITH OTHERS

 ## TALKING ABOUT JESUS

Can you remember a time when your heart burned within you when you met Jesus in the Scriptures (Luke 24:32)? Ask your parents about when they also experienced this.

 ## LISTENING TO JESUS

Sermon Title

Sermon Verse

Sermon Notes

What did you learn about Jesus today in church?

MEETING 49 | JESUS FEEDS

If you had been deserted by all your friends at your lowest moment, do you think you would want to cook them breakfast? Well, that's what we see Jesus doing when he meets them on the shore. But he does more than fill their stomachs. He also restores and repairs their souls.

TALKING TO JESUS: PRAYER POINTS

REMEMBERING JESUS: MEMORY VERSE | JOHN 20:31

MONDAY | Jesus Is the Christ

 John 20:30–31

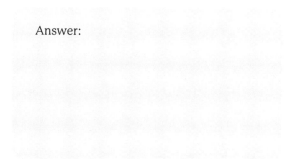 Answer:

 Why did John write his Gospel (v. 31)?

TUESDAY | Jesus Appears to His Disciples

 John 21:1–6

Answer:

 Where did Jesus appear to his disciples (v. 1)?

WEDNESDAY | Jesus Calls His Disciples to Breakfast

 John 21:7–11

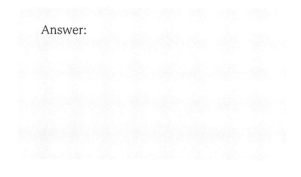 Answer:

 What did Peter do when he saw Jesus (v. 7)?

THURSDAY | Jesus Cooks Breakfast

 John 21:12–14

 How many times had Jesus appeared to his disciples after his resurrection (v. 14)?

Answer:

FRIDAY | Jesus Restores Peter

 John 21:15–19

 What did Jesus ask Peter (v. 16)?

Answer:

SATURDAY | Jesus Is Bigger Than the Bible

 John 21:20–25

John 21:25

Answer:

SUNDAY | MEETING JESUS WITH OTHERS

 ## TALKING ABOUT JESUS

Would John be happy with your response to the gospel (John 20:31)?

 ## LISTENING TO JESUS

Sermon Title

Sermon Verse

Sermon Notes

What did you learn about Jesus today in church?

MEETING 50 | JESUS ASCENDS

We've met Jesus in many ways, in many places, at many times over the past year. But he's about to ascend to heaven and disappear out of sight for many years. Let's watch him go.

 TALKING TO JESUS: PRAYER POINTS

 REMEMBERING JESUS: MEMORY VERSE | ACTS 1:11

MONDAY | Jesus Opens the Understanding

 Luke 24:44–49

Answer:

 What was to be preached (v. 47)?

TUESDAY | Jesus Commissions His Disciples

 Matthew 28:16–20

Answer:

 What were Christ's disciples to do (vv. 19–20)?

WEDNESDAY | Jesus's Life Summarized

 Acts 1:1–3

Answer:

 What did Jesus give to the disciples (v. 2)?

THURSDAY | Jesus Baptizes with the Holy Spirit

 Acts 1:4–8

 What will be the source of the disciples' power (v. 8)?

Answer:

FRIDAY | Jesus Ascends to Heaven

 Acts 1:9–11

 What accompanied Jesus to heaven (v. 9)?

Answer:

SATURDAY | Jesus Inspires Fellowship and Prayer

 Acts 1:12–14

 What did the disciples do when they went back to Jerusalem (v. 14)?

Answer:

SUNDAY | MEETING JESUS WITH OTHERS

 ## TALKING ABOUT JESUS

Although Jesus is back in heaven, we have learned how we can still meet him through the Bible, through preaching, and through fellowship with God's people. Also, as our memory verse taught us this week, we will meet Jesus face to face when he comes back to this earth at the end of time. What are you doing to prepare for that meeting?

LISTENING TO JESUS

Sermon Title

Sermon Verse

Sermon Notes

What did you learn about Jesus today in church?

MORE MEETINGS?

If you enjoyed meeting Jesus in the Gospels, why don't you now try *Exploring the Bible: A Bible Reading Plan for Kids*? It's a one-year Bible reading plan that covers the most important chapters in the whole Bible. It will not only help you to get a good understanding of the whole story of God's salvation in the Bible, but it will also show you how you can meet Jesus from the beginning to the end of the Bible.